I Believe

A Confession Book

MELVINA PEKA

© Copyright 2019-Melvina Peka. All rights reserved. No part of this publication reproduced, distributed, or transmitted in any form or by any means, or stored in a database or retrieval system unless written permission from the Author.

For worldwide distribution. Printed in Australia.

www.melvina.global

ask@melvina.global

Scripture quotations marked (ESV) are from the ESV® Bible (The Holy Bible, English Standard Version®), copyright © 2001 by Crossway, a publishing ministry of Good News Publishers. Used by permission. All rights reserved."

Scriptures are used from the

 marked NIV, taken from the Holy Bible New International Version ® NIV ® Copyright ©

1973, 1978, 1984, by

International Bible Society Used by permission of Zondervan. All rights reserved worldwide.

Scripture quotations marked NKJV, taken from the New King James Version Copyright © 1982 by Thomas Nelson. Used by permission. All rights reserved.

Scripture quotations marked (GNT) are from the Good News Translation in Today's English Version-Second

Edition Copyright © 1992 by American Bible Society. Used by Permission

Please note I have purposely not capitalized the word 'satan', as I prefer not to him any importance in my life or my book.

Disclaimer: All information contained in this publication is designed to provide helpful information on the subjects discussed on and is not in any way intended as a substitute for individual advice. The reader should seek their own professional advice in matters relating to their health and well-being.

The intent is to offer information and choices, recognizing that we are all individuals with our own viewpoints and circumstances. Should any reader choose to make use of the information contained therein, this is their choice. The publisher, companies or author disclaims any liability, loss or risk, personal or otherwise, to any person reading or following the information or applying the contents in this book.

Table of Contents

Introduction 1

Three times a day daily confessions, meditations and
declarations – take them more often as necessary. 26

Authors Note 79

About the Author 83

Introduction

I *Believe* is a book of encouragement and affirmation that can be declared over any situation at any time and is based on the Word of God, the Bible.

I wrote this book when all hell had broken loose in my life and I felt totally alone and in fear of my future.

Although I told myself that what God had spoken over me would come true no matter what my circumstances looked like but deep down in my heart, I had trouble believing and putting my faith into action. It is one thing to be able to quote the scriptures of the Bible, but believing it to be the Word of God and applying it to personal circumstances by faith is another thing because when situations turn in our lives from bad to worse, when troubles arise from every angle, when we suffer unexpected loses, then we find ourselves secretly questioning our calling and doubting the Word of God, wondering if He ever was going to respond to our prayers. We are uncertain if it was indeed God who spoke to our heart and slowly begin to lose courage. I struggled to embrace faith when things became difficult in my life. It appeared easier to give up than hold onto the promises of God when my circumstances seemed to get worse rather than better. It was easier to believe the lies of satan expressing to me that if God had loved me than I wouldn't be enduring such hardship and relentless troubles. I didn't know how to adjust my thought patterns and stop my mind from dwelling on my past failures and insecurities. The whispers from my past were influencing my mindset and lying to me that I was not good enough, that I was a disappointment and a failure. Storms of failure can come suddenly like a tsunami in our lives, destroying everything with its immense force, leaving us empty and forlorn. Health issues, marriage and relationship breakdown, loss of jobs, all can come crumbling down in a matter of minutes, and in the darkest hour of our lives, we can hear satan's tormenting voice whispering, "Where is your God now, does He not care?" What do you do when the storm is raging outside and like a boat, your life is tossing to and fro and Jesus is sleeping in the boat?

You get up and speak to that storm, telling it to be quiet and peace to be still in Jesus Name!

Storms come without warning, one moment all may be well, you are loving life and thanking God for His goodness, then suddenly one phone call, one email, one text message, one sudden diagnosis from a random medical check-up, one unexpected communication can destroy everything and bring you so low in your mind that you are unable to pull yourself back up. Job in the book of Job in the Bible went through similar sudden disasters. He lost his entire livelihood including his children and health, yet he remained unwavering in his praise to God. God remains the same as He was yesterday when He blessed us and today when we are in trouble. He does not change with times or seasons. Good days or bad days, He remains the same powerful awesome God, the chain breaker, way maker, rides on cherubim, His voice penetrates through the ocean beds and cuts through the bone and marrow, slices through the darkness and brings down kings and Queens. He roars and the foundation of the earth shudders, the ocean waves curl up, Manna falls from the sky, mouths of lions and tiger's slams shut, and the sun and the moon stands still. He appears in the fiery furnace, He is the master of the wind and the storm, He speaks, and the storm obeys, He commands, and the raven brings food to feed His chosen one, His Word is heard even in beds of hell. He hasn't lost control just because you have hit rock bottom, or your boat has capsized against a storm. He expects us to speak to the storm and walk on water. He wants us to focus on Him and not on the storm. He wants us to be led by His Spirit and not what we see. If we want greater things in life, then failures and setbacks are part of the journey. They don't come to destroy us; they come to push us out of our comfort zone toward our destiny. We were not born just to breathe air and live a purposeless life. We are called for a purpose, to do the Will of God who is our Heavenly Father, to tend the earth and multiply (see Genesis).

His promises do not change with times; nor does He alter His Words once spoken out of His mouth. He has said it and it is established forever. He told us to trust Him no matter what comes against us. It may be difficult to stay strong when our heart is breaking, when we are facing betrayal at its worse, through the foolish choices we have made and through the abandonment but we are not the only ones who have had to live through the pain of losses. Jesus walked the path before us. He was wounded for our transgressions and bruised for our iniquities. His Heavenly Father who had the power to help Him stood quiet as He went through a public trial for sins He did not commit and was beaten and hung on a cold hard wooden cross, his bloody and naked body displayed in front of all his followers while they looked on. Jesus had the power to call a multitude of angels to help Him, but He too gave up that right for you and me. He died a sinner, a rapist, a betrayer, a sick and a diseased person, a murderer, He became our sin. At some point on the cross, He became you and me with all our shame, our bad choices, our sicknesses and diseases, our guilt and wrongdoings, every sin we have not committed yet, and He took them all.

Maybe you too were falsely accused, discriminated against, criticized and shamed, stood alone and shed bitter tears while those you trusted looked on and you wondered why you had to suffer such injustice, why God would allow His children to go through hardship and trials?

When we are a new Christian we are under the false impression that Christianity is glamorous, we wear a cross and walk on an emotional high till we are hit with a terrible loss, suffer injustice and pain, go through a series of trials then we realize that being a Christian is not all that, it is hard work. Being a Christian does not exempt us from the attacks of satan in spiritual warfare where our faith is put on trial. God allows us to go through extensive training, situations that stretch our spiritual, physical and mental abilities in preparation for what is coming ahead. My own child died as I looked on, feeling helpless and hopeless, my parents died young and in my anguish I questioned God. One thing I do know is that God is all-merciful and gives us many chances and does not punish us with ill health or accidents and problems just because we have made mistakes or bad choices. It is man's way of thinking that God punishes us because of our sin or something we have done wrong to displease Him. I believe that when we make the wrong choice and do wrong things, it automatically opens a door, a passage for the devil to bring consequences. And when we repent, that passage closes.

However in Hebrews 12:7-11 (NIV) it says: "Endure hardship as discipline."

"No discipline seems pleasant at the time, but painful. Later on, however, it produces a harvest of righteousness and peace for those who have been trained by it."

If God has called us His children then He has a right to discipline us. Everyone undergoes discipline. Moreover, we have all had human fathers who disciplined us and we respected them for it. How much more should we submit to our Heavenly Father and live!

No good parent takes preference to discipline their children. We love our children, and our heart is sad when we have to correct them with a penalty when they have repeatedly done the wrong thing. How many mothers out there would agree with me that they have at some point secretly cried once they had disciplined their child and fathers hide in the shed feeling bad? That is the love of parents who want the best for their children and desire to set a strong foundation in them. We want them to grow and learn from their mistakes and prepare them for adulthood when they will be faced with bigger challenges and difficult decisions. I remember my own childhood where my mum disciplined us more than my dad. Yes, like everyone else, at that time I did not like it. But now looking back, I cannot be more grateful because it set a solid foundation for my later years. My mum did not discipline me because she hated me or took a yearning to punish me. Her corrections prepared me, nourished me BECAUSE SHE LOVED ME. She had the experience of hardship herself and understood that in life many challenges would come, that I would have to make some hard-hitting decisions and she equipped me by correcting me early in love. It was her way of showing me right from wrong. Many heroes in the Bible were flogged, beheaded, stoned, shipwrecked and imprisoned. They believed till the end that God was merciful and full of love. Job said (23:10), "When He has tested me, and I will come forth as gold." No one was tested as much as Job who had lost everything he owned and loved, not because he had done something erroneous but because God held him up to satan in a Heavenly meeting. Job, whose empire extended from real estate to agricultural holdings, who owned thousands of livestock, a myriad of servants, suddenly lost everything, yet he stood tall in God, refraining from accusing Him.

This was a God-fearing good, honest and reliable man who had not only lost all his businesses but all his children as well and his health just like that. Disaster came unexpectedly on him. He did not make corrupt business decisions, his children were not sick, he was healthy, and the Bible says, he lived a godly life. Why a good man who upheld Gods guidelines, led a truthful life, go through such adversity and trial? Where many of us would have complained, questioned and became angry with God, Job continued to worship despite he loses. Abraham in the Bible, who had a great wealth, whom God had blessed with an abundance of livestock, servants, houses, longed for a child to love and hold, an heir to his empire. He remained childless until he was old and grey when God decided to bless him. Naomi in the Bible had migrated to a distant land with her husband and two sons with high hopes and dreams of a better life, returned to her homeland empty-handed having buried her loved ones in a foreign soil. When she left her homeland, fleeing from the famine, her bosom was full. Little did she know that she would return someday without them? Devastated from her loss, with bitter pain and shattered dreams, she set out in search of a new beginning. Today you have health and wealth because God's mercy is upon you. Never cease to be humble and give God glory because you don't know what is before you around the corner. Hannah had the love of her husband, but she was childless. Her husband's other wife tormented her with harsh words till Hannah could not take it anymore and set out to seek God about her situation. With heaviness of her heart and longing in her soul, she approached God's altar and travailed in prayer and supplication, refusing to depart till He heard her prayers and opened her womb. She did not care if bystanders called her a lousy drunk or criticized her way of worship, all she knew was that she was a desperate woman with a desire greater than anything else she wanted. A dream only God could fulfil and no one else's validation or endorsement mattered to her. According to the gospel of Luke1:5-7, the Bible narratives that Elizabeth who was Mary the mother of Jesus' cousin and her husband Zachariah were righteous and blameless before God, upheld all the commandments of the Lord (1:6–7), did all their religious duties and holy tasks yet their prayer of having a child remained unanswered. This shows that our holy religious tasks, lighting candles in the church every Sunday, giving to the poor, cannot buy us points with God. God is not impressed by our charity donations, religious duties, and contributions. Faith is the only thing the Bible says that pleases Him. There are many other heroes in the Bible who did not give up hope despite their hardships, trials, and circumstances but continued to run the race against all odds. What do you do when you have believed God, trusted in Him, prayed and offered all your sacrifices but still ended up losing everything you held close to your heart and God remained silent? God is not moved by emotions but by our faith. God says even before we open our mouths to pray, He will answer (Isaiah 64:24). He cannot answer unless we pray.

Prayer is a weapon God has given to us to use to dismantle and destroy the shackles that bound us. There is no perfect prayer; prayer is simply the worship of God before you see an answer. Prayer is speaking the Word of God by faith and believing that it will manifest just like when God says it.

The Bible says; "Likewise the Spirit helps us in our weakness. For we do not know what to pray for as we ought, but the Spirit himself intercedes for us with groaning too deep for words", Romans 8:26 ESV.

When our heart is full and our tears become our prayer, the Holy Spirit intercedes for us and whatever we bind on earth is bound in Heaven and whatever we loose on earth is loosed in Heaven (Matthew 18:18). Troubles and challenges come to all of us regardless of how much we pray, go to church or read the Bible. Unless we speak the Word in the authority of the Name of Jesus believing that it will manifest, nothing will change in our lives. How we react to the troubles that come to us does matter because only when we are squeezed, we can bring about worship at a sacrificial level. It wasn't Hannah's barrenness that brought her to her knees before God; it was the constant taunting of her enemy (1 Samuel) that pushed her to her destiny. Sometimes we need the enemy to direct us to the right path, to push us out of our comfort zone. The lady with the Alabaster Jar in the Bible (Matthew 26:7), brought her sacrifice to Jesus and worshipped Him only when she became desperate for more than what life had given to her. Her lifestyle working as a prostitute did not fulfil her, it left her empty with a deep longing for something no man could give her but Jesus. No one can push us before God better than the enemies, because when we are weak, God is strong in us (2 Corinthians 12).

Storms in life have a way of clearing the debris and making a way for our destiny.

We all are searching for happiness, for peace and purpose. Even those who do not believe in God are consumed with the search of inner peace, the kind that has the potential to permeate deep inside through the trials and heartaches.

Even though I told myself that what God had spoken over me was more than enough for my victory to manifest but I had trouble believing it deep down in my heart in the middle of a crisis. I doubted His calling for my life, and I questioned His Word spoken over me. Some days I was up there high in faith and other days I was down in the dumps sceptical and speaking disbelieve negative destructive words.

I was desperate for a change in my life. I needed to transform my thought pattern, change my poverty mentality, get out of the meaningless job that was leaving me unfulfilled, become somebody, and leave a legacy. I wanted to be successful but did not understand the notion that my success and God's were not the same. I had enough of living in scarcity all the time. I wanted more out of life. If God said that He would care for me in 1 Peter 5: 7, to cast all my cares onto Him, then why was I worried about my bills and mortgage? Didn't He say in John 14:1, "Let not your heart be troubled", to give all to Him and don't worry about anything?

He said to ask boldly, to approach Him as His child and He will give me what I asked (Matthew 7:7). Then why was I sceptical, chanting on harmful negative disputes because what we speak out, manifests in our lives?

Are you like I was, troubled with anxieties of life, living in lack, heart burdened because of bad choices, troubles that threaten to overcome you, take away your joy and peace, feeling unfulfilled?

God says you and I are His children in Galatians 3:26; Adopted through the blood of Jesus into the family of God as the Jews in Ephesians 1:5-6, that means we are God's business to feed and clothe. He took you and me under His wings like a bird or a child. As His children, we have some rights. If we don't know our rights, we will live a life lesser than our calling and the devil loves to keep us in the dark about what rightfully belongs to us as children and heir of God.

I pray that His peace overtakes you today in whatever you are going through (Philippians 4:6-7). May He show you His glory as He showed Moses.

My heart was troubled; I had many unanswered questions about my life and my circumstances. What is the best place than the Bible to find answers to your troubling heart? I searched for scriptures that related to my circumstances so that I could apply them like medicine given by the physician for an ailment. I started to speak them out loud over my body, my sicknesses, over my issues and over the lives of my loved ones, instead of speaking disbelief and doubt. I refused to go through the same route another year with the same mindset and achieve nothing. I was mourning on the inside for something I could not even understand, perhaps like Jeremiah who was weeping for the people who had lost their way (Jeremiah 10:23). I knew there was more for me but didn't quite know how to find it, how to tap into the goodness of God. I desired to build my house on the rock where the storms and the pressures of life could not bring down. God says unless the Lord builds our house, we labor in vain who builds it (Psalm 127). When we invite Him in our lives and our homes, He builds it.

I had a kind of innate hunger that nothing was able to fill.

I set out to carefully choose my words. It wasn't easy when you have been accustomed to speaking your mind. Words are alive and powerful, and they can either build or destroy. The Bible says in Genesis, that God created the entire world with words. God created human beings with words. God spoke, and it was.

Since we are made in God's image, we can also use words just like He did to create, to build, to restore and to make it work for us. The Bible speaks of the tongue, being so little but having the absolute power to destroy just like a speck of fire that can sweep through a vast territory in minutes destroying everything.

The tongue has the power of life and death (Proverbs 18:21), it can either add to sorrow or remove sorrow. Kind words spoken in a timely manner can give life and peace. Words spoken harshly, in a cruel manner can destroy the heart and rob us of peace.

Word of God spoken out loud can bring us out of afflictions and add peace to our soul.

"Many are the afflictions of the righteous, but the Lord delivers him out of them all" – Psalm 34:19

The devil does not discriminate. Beautiful face, nice figure, being smart, talents, money in the bank, mansions don't matter to him.

He will continue to attack anyone who is for God. He is the enemy of God being deposed from his position as an angel of light.

Troubles do not come because we have been good or bad, or that God wants to punish us. He made us powerful just like Himself and crowned us with glory and honor and placed everything under our feet (Hebrews 2). He gave us an authority on earth, full control, in charge of everything under the sun and told us to look after it, enjoy and multiply. This makes satan very angry that God gave us such honor, importance, and much love. Devil will do everything and anything to get us to give up on God, and even if we do, God has promised never to leave us nor forsake us. He took the time to make us, knit our body parts carefully and breathed His own breath of life into us. He made us like Himself, creator, passionate, loving, gentle yet powerful. He has given us all a gift, something that only we can do and no one else can do it better than us. When we walk in His purpose, we can be all that He has called us to be.

Jeremiah wrote in the Bible, "Before I formed you in your mother's womb, I knew you. Before you were born, I set you apart and appointed you," Jeremiah 1:5 NIV.

You and I are not a mistake. It does not matter under what circumstances we were conceived and where we were found. God knew us before we were conceived in our mother's womb and that He appointed us for a specific purpose. There is nothing we can do to disappoint or surprise God and nothing we can do that He is not already aware of. God is not angry with you. He knows everything about you, your past, your present and your future and He continues to love you unconditionally. Whether you are good, or bad, it does not change His love for you. God looks at the bigger picture and does not keep an account of the little mistakes we make every day nor does He take pleasure in punishing us. His grace is enough to cover us.

You and I were on Jesus' mind when He took His very last breath. He called your name as He gave up His breath telling you that you are worth it. You were purposely made, created lovingly, knit together in the darkest place in the womb- Psalm 139:13, 14 NIV, "For you created my inmost being; you knit me together in my mother's womb. I praise you because I am fearfully and wonderfully made."

Every day we go through challenges at home, at school, and at work, in our bodies and our minds, and often we take it silently as if it was our punishment from God for doing something to offend Him. We take it as if it is our portion. This is a lie from the very pits of hell.

When the storms of life rage its fury against us and its huge waves crash on the walls of our relationships, health and finances, and when everything we built starts to crumble under its pressure, we find ourselves alone and lost, accusing God. When the skies turn grey and when our prayers don't seem to get answered and help does not come soon enough, we turn our face away from God, looking at the world for answers.

Like in the Book of Job in the Bible, although God may allow the enemy to put our faith on trial, He always has a greater purpose behind it that we may not understand. He never abandons us and has promised to restore us to a greater height. His Word (Jesus) was sent to bring healing and restoration to us from all our pain, diseases and all our troubles.

Psalm 107:20 NIV, "He sent out His Word and healed them."

It is already a done deal. Jesus exchanged His very life for our life. He took on His body all the sins of the world, all our past, present, and future sins, all our diseases, poverty, shame and everything under the curse so that we could walk away free from it all. When a person dies, they usually leave a Will. Jesus died and in His last Will and Testament, it says we have the earth and everything therein, we have the victory from sin and shame, and from every sickness and diseases and by His stripes we have been made whole. Some of us may not have read

His last Will and Testament in Bible in Ephesians 2: 14-16, Jesus' resurrection broke down the dividing wall between God and us that's why the curtain in the temple tore from the top to the bottom when He gave up His breath.

We were at fault, but God's mercy saved us all. Jonah in the Bible knew full well of God's heart, that He is quick to forgive, that is why he ran away from his assignment. He could not give us full punishment because of His eminent love for us. None the less someone had to pay that price, so God orchestrated a plan that involved His son Jesus to divert the punishment from us to Himself (1 John 4:10).

Jesus didn't stay dead. He rose up from the dead and reconciled our relationship back with the father God. He took back from satan what he stole in the garden of Eden and gave our authority on earth back as it was supposed to be at the beginning of time.

Jesus' life was on the altar in exchange for yours and my life! -Matthew 27:32-56.

Matthew illustrates in chapter twenty-seven, verse fifty, that Jesus death was a profound event as never seen or heard ever; where even the foundations of the earth had shuddered, and the rocks had split in half, tombs were opened as Jesus cried out with a loud voice and let go of his spirit as a sinful human being. Even the curtains of the temple were ripped from the top to the bottom just as Jesus flesh was ripped open. The curtain had separated sinful people from the Holy presence of God as described in Hebrews 10:20-22. Jesus flesh breaking and His blood pouring secured the reconciliation between God and us. God canceled all the debt that satan held against us on that gruesome day on the cross of Calvary in Colossians 2: 24.

Every drop of his blood that day on the cross of Calvary wiped our sinful past, present and future clean – Isaiah 53:4

Galatians 3:13 has confirmed that when Jesus died, He redeemed us all human beings from the curse of the law by Himself becoming a curse for us and God publicly endorsed Him when He rose up from the dead by giving Him a Name above all Names. And when we speak the Name of Jesus, every knee *must* bow, and every tongue must confess that Jesus Christ is Lord over everything, including sicknesses, diseases, lack, poverty and everything that has a name. The Bible says no one can come to the Father God except through Jesus. Jesus became the gateway to God, a bridge we can walk through to go to the Father's presence- John 14:6. Philippians 2:10.

No longer can satan go to God and condemn us with his lies because Jesus was already condemned for us (Romans 8:1).

He became human for you and me suffering, hurting and in agony as our sins transferred onto Him while His Heavenly Father turned His face away. When I try to imagine this scenario, my heart sings out in praise, my lips cry out in worship. Therefore healing, prosperity, peace, and restoration are already a done deal. Simply believe it and declare it over your circumstances, over your body and every sickness, over your lives and walk away free. If we don't know the rightful inheritance Jesus gave us at His death, the devil will keep us in the dark believing that we deserve the sickness and the lack.

Sometimes it appears like we are the only ones going through troubles while others seem to get on with their lives. If situations seemingly appear like a mountain too big to move and there seems to be no answer to your prayers, then this little book is for you. Whatever you are going through right now, may it be a relationship issue, or diagnosis of a disease, maybe it is your children and loved ones who are going through trying times, maybe you are about to lose your house or your job -this book will help you stay focused and anchored in Christ who is your foundation and your rock, while you worship your way out.

I have been through many challenges where I almost gave up. I was about to take my own life, but God sent help at the right time when there was no hope for me. The devil sent diseases that threatened to kill me, but God sent His Word and healed me. Broken, beaten and homeless, when all seemed too hard and impossible, His Word became my only hiding place.

I am hoping that these scriptures that I wrote during those turbulent times of my life help you as it has helped me overcome.

I would escape lunchtime to sit in the car to meditate on these scriptures because I was fed up of the devil taking from me that which was rightfully mine. It felt like I was in a mental war that was refusing to end. I wanted peace and joy in my life. If the spoken Word could work for the centurion's servant (Luke 7:1-10), then it was good enough for me. I kept them on my phone, so I could access it easily and meditate on it readily. When you are desperate you will do anything to get your healing, your relationship restored or your children back from the bondage of addictions.

No one else will do it for you. You will have to fight the good fight of faith alone for those you love. God had to sacrifice the life of Jesus so that you and I could go free. You and I are not going to sit idle and breathe the air and say, "Oh well, it is God's will that I have cancer or diabetes or lung disease because He must be punishing me for something from my past life. It must be my karma." That is a lie from the devil himself. We must speak to that sickness or that problem, "Not on God's watch, you cannot have my children, you cannot have my health, I rebuke you in Jesus Name." It is God's will that you prosper and be in health (3 John 1:2).

We have to fan that fire in our belly and rise up in faith and say to the devil, "No more, you will no longer steal from me my inheritance, health, and wellbeing." Prosperity is your inheritance, take it by force. Tell the devil, "I know who I am in Christ Jesus and I have come to take my stuff back that you stole, in Jesus Name I come satan, move aside as I take my children back home, as I take my healing back, my identity back, as I take my relationship back."

I cannot go through a day without meditating Scriptures from the Bible as if my life depended on it because every day my children, my husband and I go out into the world that is confused and take up to shooting or killing, we are surrounded by challenges that threaten to take away everything that we value because we are a chosen generation, a royal priesthood (1 Peter 2:9), and God has called us His children and we are in the wanted list of satan.

It is my way of life now, that I declare the Word of God over every situation in my life and that of my loved ones.

I find hope and comfort in the Word of God and it helps me to remain calm when everything is breaking around me in the storm. I am hoping that your words will match Gods words bringing you peace and restoration.

Many leave their homes to go to work and do not return but because of His protection and His blood shed for me and my loved ones; we come home safely each day. Even when we have made the most horrible mistake and have lost everything, our God Jehovah does not cast us away from His sight. He scoops us up from the deep dark hole like a strong eagle and places us on a high rock.

David in the Bible suffered many challenges and made many mistakes, but he found a way to the heart of God through worship. These Words are Gods Words and when you speak them out loud; your worship will bring God into your situation wherever you are.

I meditate on these scriptures when I am struggling with mountains that are too big for me.

These scriptures have been my daily medicine, giving me life and a right to live again. His love took away my shame. The Word comes alive in my situation as I prayerfully speak it loudly. Speak it over your children and grandchildren, believing that it will manifest.

This book is small enough to be carried in your handbag. Personalize it and meditate it till it comes alive in your heart and soul and then it will manifest in the flesh.

John 14:14 says if we ask anything in His name, He will do it. So, ask, and He will do it!

Write your asks or your requests here:

Three times a day daily confessions, meditations and declarations – take them more often as necessary.

Put your children's or loved one's names in the blanks and meditate on them three or more times a day as you like. You cannot overdose on the Word medicine of God.

Write down here your needs, what you are praying for, you ask of God, find a believer who can come in AGREEMENT with your prayer and lay your hands over it prayerfully speaking the Name of Jesus and asking for mercy and help. He cannot answer unless you pray.

Matthew 18:19-20 KJV, "Again I say unto you, that if two of you shall agree on earth as touching anything that they shall ask, it shall be done for them of my Father which is in heaven."

_____

_____

I Believe

I say that the Word of God is alive and penetrates through every cell of my body, through the bone and marrow, my eyes and my vision, and every fiber, nerve and organs and brings healing as I speak it out loud because Gods Word cannot return to Him empty. "For the word of God is alive and active, sharper than any double-edged sword. It penetrates even to dividing soul and spirit, joints and marrow; it judges the thoughts and attitudes of the heart. Nothing in all creation is hidden from God's sight. Everything is uncovered and lay bare before the eyes of him to whom we must give account." - Hebrews 4:12

The Bible says in Proverbs 3:8 that the Word, will be healing to your flesh and refreshment to your bones. It will be health to your navel, and marrow to your bones. This is when we apply the Word of God in our lives by meditating and believing that it has the power to heal and restore; to bring to life dead hopes and dreams in our lives.

Meditations and declarations:

Romans 12:16, James 1:17; 1 Peter 4:10, Matthew 6:33, Proverbs 18:16, 2 Corinthians 9:8.

Every good and perfect gift is from God. These gifts and talents that God has given to me are mine and no one can snatch it away from me. As I speak it out loud, His promises over me are opening a way for me. I take steps out of my comfort zone. It might look fearful, but I declare that God has not given to me a spirit of fear but one of power and a sound mind; therefore, I call upon God's wisdom and courage and take these steps without fear because God is beckoning me and like Peter, I will step out of the boat. I will step out of my fears and walk toward Jesus to my destiny.

I make a purposeful decision and choose this day to pursue God with all that is within me because His Word says, seek you first the Kingdom of God and His righteousness and He will give me all good things.

I believe according to His Word that as I use the gifts and talents that He has given to me, it will put me in the right place and usher me into the presence of great men and women who will show me a favor.

My children's (put your loved ones names here), gifts and

talents are creating a way for them to success, for it is written that all things abound to those that love the Lord and are called to His purpose.

2 Corinthians 9:8, Proverbs 10:22

My children will find their purpose as they take this step forward in Jesus Name. I declare and prophesy in the powerful Name of Jesus in whose Name every knee must bow. Every obstacle will be removed as I advance in Jesus Name.

It is written that God can make all grace overflow to me and His blessing makes me rich and adds no sorry to it. I declare today that the Grace of God overtakes me in Jesus Name, and I walk in His blessing and righteousness all the days of my life; my going out and my coming in remains blessed to full measure and overflowing.

Luke 6:38; Exodus 23:19

Lord, I thank you that I am never without a seed to plant into your Kingdom. I will always have something that I can use to give like a farmer and my harvest will be abundant and never run out. I believe by faith that the seeds that I have planted in good soil will produce a rich harvest in my life to overflowing through generations to come. Your word says to give and it shall be given unto me full measure pressed down; shaken together and running over shall men give unto my bosom and to try you now and see if you will not open the windows of heaven and pour me out such a blessing that I will not have enough room to contain it. I receive this in Jesus Name.

Jeremiah 30:17, Job 42:10, Joel 2: 25, 26, Psalm 23, Psalm 71: 20-24, Isaiah 35:4-6

My Heavenly Father, you have said that you will restore unto me everything that the enemy has stolen. My vision and my hearing will be restored. Today I declare that my health is returned unto me. I speak life to all my body parts, my organs, my finances, and my relationships. I call opportunities to be opened unto me and lost opportunities will be restored.

As I speak your Word, you are restoring unto me more than I lost.

I believe the restoration of all my money, my families, my time and my moments, my health and wellbeing and I shut the door to the enemy. My eyesight is restored, my memory is restored, my knee is restored, my limbs are restored, and my health is restored in Jesus Name.

Psalm 71:20-21, Galatians 3:13, Deuteronomy 28, Romans 3:23

You have allowed me to suffer much hardship, but you will also restore me to life again and lift me up from the depths of the earth. You will restore me to even greater honor and comfort me once again. God as you restored

Job to much more than he had lost, you will also restore me as well, to a higher place, a better place than I was previously. My health will be restored so that your name will be glorified in my life. You will show me how to get out of debt and owe to no man because I ask for wisdom and knowledge that only you can give and the power to gain wealth and success in all I do.

Romans 4:17, Matthew 18:19, Deuteronomy 28, Matthew 18:19

Father God, you give life to the dead and speak things to come into motion with your Word, I now speak to all those things that be dead in my life, things that I have given up hope, to come to life. My name shall be put forward before someone of power because your word says that I am highly favored of you. When I am favored in your sight then I am favored in the sight of others around me.

In Jesus Name whose Name is above every name, I declare the Blessing of Abraham to surround me and my children, and my loved ones. I agree with my husband/wife/friend over this issue:

because it is written if two of us agree on earth on anything that we ask then it will be done for us by our Father in heaven. In Jesus Name we believe we receive it. Amen.

Galatians 5:1; Proverbs 6:31, John 8:36, Proverbs 6:31

I take authority over you satan and bind you the spirit of death and destruction, the spirit of lack and poverty, the spirit of hindrance and generational curses in my life and in the lives of (put the names of your children here), in the mighty name of Jesus. I plead the blood of Jesus over myself and over my children

By the blood of Jesus and by His word I am/we are set free. For it is written whomever the Son sets free are free indeed. I demand you satan, all things stolen from me, from my children, from my ancestors be returned to us 7-fold immediately right now right here for it is written when the enemy is caught, he must return 7-fold!

Philippians 1:6, Proverbs 28:1, 1Peter 4:11, Philippians 4:13, Proverbs 28:1

I declare that what God has assigned for me is mine. No one can take it away from me and no one else can do it better than me. I step on fear and take steps toward my destiny. I am confident in myself because I see myself in the eyes of Jesus and not in my own abilities.

Zechariah 4:6, Isaiah 60, 61, Luke 4:18, Luke 10:19, Proverbs 16:3

It is not in my own ability but only by the spirit of God signs and wonders follow me wherever I go, in Jesus name Amen.

It is written that the blind will see, the dead will rise, and the demons will flee in Jesus name as I declare the Word of God. Success follows me wherever I go. I say what it is for God has given me the authority to use the Name of Jesus and signs and wonders follow me.

<u>1 John 4:4, Genesis 22:17, Matthew 4:1-11, Deuteronomy 28:6, Psalm 121:8, 2 Corinthians 9:8</u>

I may have been led into the wilderness, but I refuse to stay here, because I am in transition, passing through this wilderness to my destiny. I refuse to allow my circumstances to speak to my destiny. My destiny has already been spoken over me by God at the beginning of time. I am the apple of God's very own eyes. I do not need anyone's permission to walk into His presence. I come to my Heavenly father boldly and fearlessly.

<u>James 4:7, 1 Peter 4:11, 2 Corinthians 9:8</u>

It is written, submit to God, resist the devil and he will flee; Father I submit to you and bring unto you all that I am and all that I ever want to be. I declare you as my Lord and my savior. I ask you to use me to expand your Kingdom and to bring you glory.

1 Peter 4:10-11, Genesis 13:15

God, you have said that as far as my eyes can see, you will give it to me. Today I declare to see my (ministry, my music album, my book, my marriage, my debt free house, my job, my children saved). Put your children's names here

I call my children out of the darkness in Jesus Mighty Powerful Name whose Name is above every addiction, every alcohol drugs, and every chain every stronghold that is holding my children back, I curse the roots of it in Jesus Name and today I declare freedom for my children. LET GO OF MY CHILDREN, MY FINANCES, MY MIND, MY HOUSEHOLD satan in Jesus Mighty Name, Amen.

I speak this in faith and I believe it is mine, in the Name of Jesus. I have spoken, and so it shall be because my words carry power to create, to build, to restore.

Psalm 126:1

I trust you, God; to place me and my children (put the names of your children and who you are praying for), in a position

_____
_____
_____
_____
_____
_____
_____
_____
_____
_____
_____
_____
_____
_____
_____
_____
_____

where we can boldly declare like the Israelite's that, "When the Lord brought back the captivity of Zion, we were like those who dream. Then our mouth was filled with laughter, and our tongue with singing. Then they said among the nations, the Lord has done great things for them, the Lord has done great things for us and we are glad." Father, I declare that I will rejoice and declare your goodness in front of all my haters because you have filled me to the brim and my cup overflows. I prophesy that your goodness will overtake us, doors will be kicked open as it did for Paul in Acts 12:5 and your angel will lead us out of debt, out of lack, out of poverty, out of troubles that have come upon us in Jesus Name. We are the head and not the tail. We fly like Eagles in high places. We have ministering angels guarding us, our going out and our coming in is protected as it says in Psalm 91.

Romans 11:29, Revelation 3:8, Isaiah 22:22

Jehovah, my Father almighty, you have promised me and my children, my grandchildren, that gifts and callings will not be withdrawn or taken away, and I declare those callings to come into existence and make a way to greater things. I thank you that it will do what you have sent it to do in my life and that of my children and through us reach millions, in Jesus Name. When the time comes, I pray and declare that I will be able to overcome every obstacle, have victory over every giant who dares to come against me and walk into my destiny because you paid the cost to my salvation and that of others. My calling and my children's calling will manifest in due time and it is here now, I receive it in Jesus mighty powerful Name.

Proverbs 1:20; Lamentations 3:23

I hear wisdom and I listen and obey. My children hear wisdom and they listen and obey. I will make the right choices and decisions that bring you glory. I will exercise wisdom and knowledge that you give me and walk in freedom from confusion.

Your word says your grace is new every morning and does not take into consideration mistakes made; I receive it in Jesus Name.

1 Timothy 4:12; John 8:36; Malachi 4:2

I boldly share the gospel of Christ with everyone God places across my path and healing takes place in everyone who listens and believes. I take authority over addictions and bondages in my life, for it is written whomever the son sets free is free indeed.

Jesus, you have said that those who revere your name, the sun of righteousness shall rise with healing in its wings and we will go free leaping with joy. Today I choose to walk away free of my addictions, my sickness, cataracts, glaucoma, heart disease, arthritis, joint pains, migraine pains, lumber, and spinal pain, (name here your sicknesses and all your issues).

for you have risen with healing on your wings over my diseases and situations. I receive by faith that every name that has taken offense in my body, in my organs, in my cells and joints, must now bow to the name of Jesus and leave. I receive my healing and restoration by faith according to the Word of God and by my confession.

2 Peter 1:3-4, Revelation 3:8

God, I believe you will send me resources for what you have called me to do and I will not lack anything and neither will I be begging from anyone because you alone supply all of my needs according to your glory and not by my own works.

When you open doors, no one can close them and when you shut doors no one can open them, so I ask you to shut those doors in my life that is not bringing you glory and open doors that take me closer to my destiny of success and prosperity as per your Word. By faith, I walk through the open-door with boldness and confidence, believing that you have opened this door for me, and no one will be able to close it. I am the only one destined to walk this path that you have opened before me. I walk with grace and boldness.

Job 8:7; Haggai 2:9, Genesis 17, Psalm 50:7-15

It is written in your Word, that my later years will be better than my former because the Lord is my God who supplies my needs accordingly to His riches in Glory by

Christ Jesus my Lord. I will not suffer any lack. I will always have plenty for myself and surplus to give away. I shall never live in want because you are my provider owning cattle on a thousand hills. Why should I fear my tomorrow because you have seen my tomorrow and command my day accordingly?

I believe by faith that I am transitioning into the better years of my life leaving my past behind to pursue the calling that is ahead of me and it is never too late for God who gave Abraham a child in his old age and renewed Sarah's youth to bless me even in my senior years. I will accomplish all that you have called me to do and not die before that. I walk in great boldness and confidence and fear nothing and no one because you alone are my fortress and my strong tower of refuge. I will not die prematurely without fulfilling my calling.

Ephesians 2:9; Proverbs 8:35, Joel 2:25, Luke 1:28

I'm highly favored of God and favor and success follows me wherever I go, because it is written whoever finds God finds life and obtains favor from the Lord. I confess that I have a long-life, walking in your favor and your goodness, and my children and grandchildren will inherit all that you have assigned for me as a generational blessing.

Psalm 5:12; Galatians 3:14; Deuteronomy 30:3

My source is not my income. My God is my source and in Him I live and breathe. I am called to live in Abraham's blessing and covenant, and I have no lack. Me, my children, my grandchildren, my spouse have a regular income for God as our source, our provider and keeper. We refuse to be in lack of anything. We have plenty, our storage is full, and we give away plenty. We are in overflow for it is written that God blesses the righteous, O Lord; you cover him with favor and with your shield.

Exodus 15:26; Exodus 23:25; Deuteronomy 7:15; Isaiah 40:28; Hebrews 6:14-20; Genesis 22:17

I declare in Jesus Name that my body is healed, for it is written, He sent His Word and healed my diseases and His Word dwells in me. I'm healthy and I'm strong for its written God renews my strength like that of an eagle, I will soar high and not get weary. I will live a long healthy life and fulfill all that God has assigned me to do on earth for it is written with blessing I will bless you, with multiplying I will multiply you and with long life I will satisfy you and show you my salvation. Fear, not I'm with you, says the Lord. I am living and laughing in His blessing and favor.

Psalm 118:17; Psalm 103:205

I will not die but live and declare the works of God. You oh Lord, have forgiven all my iniquities and pardoned all my sins. You have healed all my diseases; redeemed my life from destruction. You have satisfied my mouth with good things so that my youth is renewed like the eagles. I will run and not get weary. My bones will not get weary, arthritis will not limit my mobility, I will live in full function of my body as God assigned at the beginning of time.

Joel 2: 25; Psalm 23:1-3; Genesis, Isaiah 38: 4-6; Psalm 103:5; Judges 14:16

Father, you have said that you will restore my youth, my life, and my soul. You promised to restore the years that the locust has eaten. You are my Shepherd; I will not lack in anything because you restore my soul. As you renewed Sarah and Rebekah's youth, you renew mine too, for I declare I am the daughter of Sarah and the seed of Abraham in Jesus Name. You restore me and add years to my life as you did Hezekiah and as you restored Job. Thank you for releasing your supernatural power into my body as you did in Sampson so that I can do mighty things you have called me to do in Jesus mighty Name and death will not touch me till I say when I want to come home to be with you.

Luke 17; Mark 11:25

The joy of the Lord is my strength and I hold no offense in my body. I forgive and let go so that new anointing can be poured into me. My body holds no offense of sickness and diseases because I forgive, and I let go and hold no grudge causing my healing to manifest in the cells of my body giving me a new life I speak in Jesus Name.

Psalm 107:20; Romans 8:11

Father, it's written, you sent your word that has penetrated through all the cells in my body, through my organs and systems and has restored and healed me. I speak your word and it releases life to my cells, fibers, joints, ligaments, bones and marrows, and organs of my body. I have the same power that raised Jesus from death and I release it by declaring it over my body systems, cells, every fiber, muscles, sinews, ligaments, bones and marrow, brain cells and systems, cervical and lumbar spine, spleen, liver, heart, muscles of the heart, hearing, memory and cognition in Jesus Name and command every offense to leave my body. I give you glory for your healing power manifested in my body and in my life now in Jesus Name Amen.

Matthew 6:33; Proverbs 3:9-10; Deuteronomy 26

Heavenly Father, you have said that if I seek first your kingdom, your ways, and your righteousness; then all blessings shall come to me and I will increase. You said you will supply all my needs according to your very own riches in glory. I believe and declare your word and it is working in my life right now in Jesus Name causing me to live in health and well-being and in peace with everyone. I close the door to every offense, every negative word spoken over me, I step over un-forgiveness and I refuse to be a slave to negative thoughts and fear. I free myself with the Words of my mouth and forgive myself and others who have offended me. I walk freely now with a clear conscience in Jesus Amen.

2 Samuel 23: 8 – 39; 1 Chronicles 11: 10-47; 1 King 18: 45, 46; Jeremiah 17: 5-8; Psalm 1: 1-3; Psalm 103; Joel 3: 10; Psalm 91

Father, you are a mighty, powerful and an awesome God who enables me to do mighty deeds in your supernatural strength and power because I can do all things in you and achieve greatness in you. I say I am strong, I am healthy, my limbs and movements are strong; I have a mind of Christ and think with clarity and have great remembrance and cognition.

I will not fall, for your angels hold me up as in Psalm 91. You lead me to green pastures and beside clear cool waters as in Psalm 23. You are with me in my old age as you were with Abraham and Elijah, and as you were with David. I do not fear anything for you are with me comforting me always. I walk in victory. You are a God of fire, burn everything in me that is not of you, the root of every sickness and disease in Jesus Name.

Philippians 4:19; Proverbs 10:22; Luke 6:36 Deuteronomy 8:18; Proverbs 3: 9, Deuteronomy 26

I call every good thing that you have for me to come in my life and the lives of my children, my grandchildren, and my spouse

_____
_____
_____
_____
_____
_____
_____
_____
_____
_____
_____
_____
_____
_____
_____
_____
_____
_____
_____
_____

I declare the wealth of the wicked to come to me as per Your Word, resources open up to me, opportunities and success come to me in Jesus Name because I have power in the words of my mouth and what I say is. I will recognize opportunities for business and success as I hear your voice in the depth of me directing me.

I declare I am born of God and elected to be the son of God by grace and I am unstoppable in all that God has called me to do. I take over businesses, lands, Kingdoms on earth as did Joshua. I am a Kingdom warrior and I say what is in my life. I take the bow and arrow of the Word of God and release it to my enemies destroying its strongholds and enemy legions' plans in my street, my town, my workplace, my home and marriage, and my country.

Lord God, you have said that when I remember the Lord my God, you will give me the power to gain wealth so that you may establish your covenant which you swore unto my father Abraham to this day. I live in my blessing and peace that you have given unto me at the beginning of time. I am blessed, protected, surrounded and protected by your favor.

Deuteronomy 28:13; Deuteronomy 26

My children and I are successful in all we do because it's written that they are the head and not the tail and great is their peace as they live in Abraham's blessing, they lack nothing. We take nations; we subdue territories and take on giants. We are a royal priesthood, a chosen generation, the greater one lives and walks in and through me. I declare the peace of God in my home and marriage and relationship with my children.

Matthew 18:18; Proverbs 6:30; Ephesians 6:12; John 16:23-24

All sickness, diseases, and debt of any kind has been removed from my life because it is written I have the power and authority of the name of Jesus to bind anything on earth and whatever I bind on earth is bound in Heaven and whatever I loose on earth is loosed in Heaven therefore I bind and remove the mortgage debt and loose finances in Jesus Name. The devil is returning 7-fold of what he has stolen from me and my children in Jesus Name I declare a full restoration. I bind the spiritual powers of darkness holding my blessing and render it harmless, useless, and powerless against me and my children and grandchildren. I am who God says I am, regardless of my circumstances, my situations, my mistakes, and my bad choices. God can restore and fix every mistake. God uses my mistakes for His Glory and for my good.

Proverbs 11:24-25; Psalm 54:4; Psalm 112:3; Proverbs 22

Father in Heaven, today I declare health and wellbeing in my house as you have said that Your righteousness endures forever in my life and in my home, for me and my household, we serve the Lord and no other.

We are born of God and called the children of God bearing your mark of righteousness.

You have said that He that has a bountiful eye shall be blessed; for I give out of my own need to the poor and the needy and you have said because I give I will increase as I withhold not from those who need. You have given me plenty so that I can be your hands and feet feeding the needy, those in captives, in jail and bring Glory to your Name.

<u>Proverbs 28: 20, Deuteronomy 28: 11-14, Luke 6:38; Proverbs 22:7</u>

I declare the word of God over my life and the lives of my children and my grandchildren; that the faithful shall abound with the blessing and the Lord shall make me have plenty in everything and in the land which the Lord swore unto my father Abraham. This is where God has led me to work, to live and I will prosper in all my ways. I have the wisdom of God and make good choices and decisions and walk in His ways and eat of the land that is plentiful.

<u>Psalm 46:1-3; 1 Samuel 16</u>

God is my refuge and strength and an everlasting help in trouble.

Father, I trust you in trouble when the world has turned against me, I will hide in your shadow. You give me the strength to face the lions in my life like David in the fields. I will not fear anybody for your Word has said that man can do nothing unto me because you are the powerful one inside of me. You are with me guiding and cheering me on. I am a king of earth; you have given me keys to rule the earth and the devil is under my feet. I now know who I am, and I will not allow the devil to fool me. I am powerful and I have the power of God residing in me. I have the weapons of faith and of your Word and that is enough to fight any battle. For you are my keeper and protector.

Mark 11:23; Proverbs 6:31; Matthew 18:18; Isaiah 60; Jeremiah 33; Mark 16:17-18; Galatians 3:13; Matthew 28:18

Jesus before you went to Heaven, you said you gave all power and authority back to me and that signs and wonders will follow me wherever I go. I believe in the power of your Name Jesus, therefore when I lay my hands on the sick, healing takes place. I lay my hand on myself and healing takes place in my body in Jesus Name.

Proverbs 18:10

God you have said that your joy is my strength, therefore, I will not give in to my feelings of sadness or depression and rejoice in your Word for your Word is giving me confidence and power to stand up to my enemies.

Joshua 1:9

God, you commanded Joshua to be strong and courageous, not to be afraid, that you are with him. I take this word and declare it in my life. I will gird my loins and be strong in your word knowing that you are with me as I go forth facing my giants today. I speak with authority and walk in confidence knowing that I am not alone in this.

Proverbs 18:10 NKJV

"The Name of the Lord is a strong tower; the righteous run into it and are safe."

Father, I declare with my mouth that you are my strong tower, my strength, and my peace and as you have called me righteous, I will run to you when I am overwhelmed, when I am feeling depressed and anxious, knowing that you will hide me in a safe place from my enemies.

2 Timothy 1:7 NIV

God your Word has said that you have not given me fear.

"For the Spirit God gave us does not make us timid, but gives us power, love, and self-discipline."

I say that I have a sound mind and self- discipline; I do not give in to flesh desire. I have peace of God. I refuse to fear. I walk in victory.

Matthew 19: 26 NIV

"Jesus looked at them and said, 'With man this is impossible, but with God all things are possible.'"

Lord God Almighty, even though my situation might look impossible and I may not have resources and support, but I trust you that you will make this possible because you don't need a man's approval or earthly resources. I trust you as my

Matthew 6:34 NIV

"Therefore, do not be worry about tomorrow, for tomorrow will worry about itself. Each day has enough trouble of its own."

I will renounce my worries, fears, and anxiety and take on the garment of peace and rest in your love knowing that my tomorrow is in your hands. I am grateful for today, for all I have is this very moment that I am in right now, and the rest is in your hands. I thank you for my 'now'. I will rejoice in it and be glad that you have given me the breath of life and the special moments of 'now'. Even though it may not be a happy place right now for me, I choose to see this as a place of worship and when I worship, even my troubles turn into a Holy ground because you descend in my worship and take a seat and where you are, oh Lord, darkness and troubles must expel. I will worship you right now.

Mark 16:15; Isaiah 60; Jeremiah 33; Romans 11:29; Revelation 3:8; Isaiah 22:22

Jesus you have commanded me to go and preach the Gospel all around the world and to lay my hands on the sick and they will recover. I declare new opportunities are being opened to me and my children in Jesus Name to minister your gospel and to bring healing to your people.

Psalm 107:20; Exodus 15:26; Matthew 8:8; Numbers 21: 8-9; 2 Kings 20:4-5

I'm the Healed; I am the restored, for He sent His Word and healed my diseases. Me, my children, are totally healed physically, spiritually, financially, mentally; body soul spirit. Father God Jehovah my provider, my maker, Your Word is enough to bring healing and restoration to my bones in Jesus Name.

2 Corinthians 8:9; Hosea 4:6; Galatians 3:13-14; Genesis 28; Deuteronomy 28; Isaiah 61:10

I'm prosperous for Jesus took away my poverty, my infirmity and given me prosperity and by His stripes, I was healed. I lack nothing because I live in Abraham's Blessing. I'm wearing His robe of righteousness and nothing can harm us. We are the chosen generation, called for a purpose and whoever fights us, is fighting God and they cannot win.

Psalm 18: 1-2 ESV

"I love you, O Lord, my strength. The Lord is my rock and my fortress, my deliverer, my God, my rock, in whom I take refuge, my shield and the horn of my salvation, my stronghold."

When the enemies come my way, they will fall, for you are my refuge and my shield, my stronghold, I shall not fear. I will sleep well without fear and anxiety, without worry about tomorrow because the ministering angels have been assigned to guard me and my household and to watch over all that which belongs to me.

Psalm 34:10 NIV

"The lions may grow weak and hungry, but those who seek the Lord lack no good thing."

Father, I have always looked at your face with all my heart and according to your powerful everlasting Word, I will lack nothing. You oversee me and provide for me.

Psalm 128:3, 52:8, 112:2, 127:3-5; 121:8; Jeremiah 18:8; Deuteronomy 28:6

My children are highly favored of God. Money is attracted to them. Their bank balance increases. They want nothing because the Blessing of Abraham belongs to them. Favor and opportunities come to them in Jesus Name. The Holy Spirit sits on them birthing God's purpose for their lives.

Isaiah 54:13

My children (write their names here)

are taught of the Lord, my offspring are blessed of the Lord, they are like trees planted by the river, their roots going deep, and they produce an abundance of fruit in due season and great is their peace in Christ Jesus.

I declare from this day forward that my children's and my needs

_____
_____
_____
_____
_____
_____
_____
_____
_____
_____
_____
_____
_____
_____
_____
_____
_____
_____
_____

are met according to God's riches in glory by Christ Jesus my Lord; our debts are paid in full and we live in total healing and restoration and in abundance in Jesus name, for Abraham's blessing is mine and my children's.

I am standing on Your Word my Lord and I'm looking to you to take care of me and my family, and pay our bills and our mortgage debt for you said you give is favor in all we do and great will be our peace. You alone are my provider my EL Shaddai my burden bearer, my strength, and my peace. My trust is in you. In Jesus Name, I declare this today, Amen

It is written that I belong to Christ then I am Abraham's seed and an heir according to the promise and I will receive what God has promised and I'm debt-free and live in total abundance in Jesus Name for God is our provider and our keeper.

<u>Deuteronomy 28: 1-13</u>

It is written, that I am blessed of the Lord, I'm blessed in the city, I'm blessed in the country. I'm blessed going out, I'm blessed coming in. I'm blessed in my barns (pantry), I'm blessed in my fields (bank balance/job/my ministry/my income, business). My husband/wife and my children and I are blessed in all the work of our hands (read out their names loud when you declare)

Isaiah 53:5, Isaiah 41:10; Psalm 107:19-21; Psalm 30:2; Proverbs 4:20-22; James 5:14; Matthew 1:28

He was wounded for my transgressions; He was bruised for my iniquities; the chastisement of my peace was upon Him and with His stripes, I was healed. Therefore I command every sickness and disease, every pain and symptoms to leave my body and the body (you can put names of diseases, i.e. cancer, heart disease) in Jesus Name and every functions of my body, every nerve, every fibre, every organ, every cell, joints, bones and ligaments, blood and cells, spine and disc; skin, ovaries; womb, prostate, heart; valves, arteries, spleen, liver, pancreas, stomach, and all the systems of my body to work in the perfection God created it to function in Jesus Name. I apply the blood of Jesus. There will be no malfunction in my body in Jesus Name. My blood pressure is normal 120/80; my heart is strong, my heart rate is normal and there is no palpitations, no malfunctions, my arteries have perfect elasticity, the valves of my heart work in the perfection of God's glory, my pancreas make the exact amount of insulin, all enzymes of my body function in its original condition as assigned by God at the beginning of time. My brain and brain cells and nervous systems and functions work perfectly as God assigned it to function, my cognition and memory are great for I have a mind of Christ. My kidneys and bladder systems, my liver, work in the perfection of God's glory. My joints, ligaments, and muscles have no pain or discomfort; arthritis will flee because the sun of righteousness shall rise with healing in His wings. For it is written, Jesus body was broken for my healing, therefore, I was healed and restored to perfect health and peace. I acknowledge and release healing in my body for it is written He sent His Word and healed my diseases. I acknowledge the power of Jesus inside of me healing and restoring me. I receive in Jesus Name. AMEN.

I call my children out of darkness to the light of Jesus (put their names here and call out loud as you declare in faith),

_____
_____
_____
_____
_____
_____
_____
_____
_____
_____
_____
_____
_____
_____
_____
_____
_____
_____
_____
_____
_____
_____

and no weapon formed against us shall prosper. I condemn every tongue that shall rise against us in judgment and bring it down into condemnation and bind the powers of the enemy in Jesus Name for it is written greater is He that is in us than he that is in the world.

I choose you Jesus over the world and over every curse spoken over me and my children. You uphold me with your righteous right hand through every situation in my life, I am never alone.

Father, you said to come to you those who are weary and burdened and you will give rest. I am in need oh Lord, as I bring you my worries and concerns that hold me in chains, give me peace and rest.

Psalm 103:2-4; Psalm 41:2-3

I will praise you Lord, and not forget all you have done for me and my children. You promised you will not give me up to my enemies.

Jeremiah 17:14; Psalm 147:3

Heal me Lord, and I will be healed. Save me and I will be saved, for you are the one I praise. Your praise shall be continually on my lips as you are my healer. You heal the broken-hearted and bind up my wounds.

Exodus 15:26; Exodus 23:25; Luke 8:49-56; Luke 8:43-48

Lord, you said you will not bring to me the curses and diseases that you brought to Egypt if I listen to you and do your word because you are the healer. You said you will take away sickness from me. You are the healer of all diseases. No one goes away from you empty-handed. Whoever comes to you finds grace in your sight.

Philippians 4:19

Father, you promised you will meet all my needs according to your wealth and glory in Jesus and not based on my work or joblessness. I trust you Lord to be my provider.

Isaiah 61; Psalm 1:2; Isaiah 61:1; Luke 4:18

He has sent me to bring good news to the poor, to heal the broken-hearted, to announce release to the captives, and freedom to those in prison.

He has sent me to proclaim that the time has come when the Lord will save His people and defeat their enemies.

He has sent me to comfort all who mourn. I go out in full confidence of the Name of Jesus and cast out demons and lay hands on the sick.

Joshua 1:8; Luke 8:49-56

This book of the law of the Lord shall not depart out of my mouth. I shall meditate upon your word day and night and it shall make my way prosperous for it is written greater is He that is in me than he that is in the world. It heals my body and restores my bones.

Psalm 37:23

God almighty Jehovah Jireh, my provider and my keeper, the rock of ages, you have said that the steps of a good man are ordered by the Lord and that you delight in his ways. Today I declare your word that you guide my steps and open doors for me and my ways delight you.

1 Peter 5:7; Psalm 4:8; Proverbs 3:24

Father you have asked me to cast all my cares onto you because you care for me, therefore, I throw all my worries, my anxieties, my depression and concerns to you and I receive your peace and joy in my life. I will go to sleep without worry for you to give your beloved good sleep.

Proverbs 3:5-6; Psalm 37:4

Father as you have asked to trust you in all decision making even though I may not know what to do, which way to go, but I trust you completely because you have a way of making even my failures, my mistakes into a blessing for me. I will lean onto you with all my heart and acknowledge your wisdom, knowledge, and guidance in this situation and believe that you will direct my path. I will delight in you and you will give me my heart's desires.

John 10:27

God my father and my provider you have said your sheep hear only your voice and know your voice well, therefore, they will not follow anyone else. I choose to follow you and hear your quiet voice guiding me in the direction you want me to go. I refuse to listen to the chatter around me.

Proverbs 18:10

Father your name is a strong tower, a shelter where I run and find safety as per your word that calls out to me. You are the tower I lean on as the waves hit me from every side. You are the anchor of my soul and I trust you will lead me safely to shore. I ask, Spirit take control, have your way in my life.

Psalm 147: 3; Isaiah 43:4; Proverbs 16:24

Father the wounds and hurts in my heart run so deep that I have not been able to forgive. Help me to forgive for you are the healer of the broken heart. Help me to see how precious I am in your sight oh Lord. I lay my anger at your feet. I will rise from this brokenness for your word says that even if I fall many times you will help me rise again.

Isaiah 43:2 NIV

"When you pass through the waters, I will be with you; and when you pass through the rivers, they will not sweep over you. When you walk through the fire, you will not be burned; the flames will not set you ablaze."

I thank you, Lord, that the situations and troubles in my life will not overwhelm me because you are with me. Their venom will not consume me.

Authors Note

Words are alive and powerful. Every word that comes out of our mouth prints a picture in our mind, a blueprint causing it to manifest. It can be both good and bad; it will do what you say.

Speak negative and see how it changes lives and those around you. Likewise, speak positive declarations and see how it changes circumstances in your life and the lives of your loved ones.

That is why people generally do not easily forget harsh words spoken over them. Years may go by and they will still remember that hurtful word spoken over them and they continue to live in bondage for the rest of their lives believing the lies of satan.

Speak only what you mean and what you want to be manifested in your life and of others. Speak purposefully and do not speak idle words. Your words shape your life.

Speak what God says over you in His word and live life to the fullest as He wants you to.

You are the very apple of His eye. You are His beloved.

We are but a lump of soil in the potter's hand; trials and challenges sculpture us till we emerge perfectly for His glorious use

If this book has helped you, please write a review so that others may get encouraged and empowered and stay anchored to God as they battle through the waves of life.

About the Author

Melvina Peka is a life coach and a motivational speaker, empowering people through her podcasts, books, and online courses.

Melvina lives in Australia with her husband and children.

Melvina came out of a domestic violence relationship which caused the death of her first child. She suffered depression and anxiety, made poor choices and suffered low self-image and confidence. God has delivered Melvina by His spoken Word.

Melvina helps other people now to fight their fears and insecurities and rise up to God's plan for their lives.

Melvina's books:

Broken to Restored; a true story of faith and healing

https://www.amazon.com/s?k=broken+to+restored+by+melvina+peka

To join Melvina Peka Ministries mailing list:

https://melvina.global/

www.ingramcontent.com/pod-product-compliance
Lightning Source LLC
Chambersburg PA
CBHW031427290426
44110CB00011B/558